THE FUTURE OF AI

AI and the Workforce

Traci Pedersen

ReferencePoint Press

San Diego, CA

Printed in the United States

For more information, contact:
ReferencePoint Press, Inc.
PO Box 27779
San Diego, CA 92198
www.ReferencePointPress.com

LIBRARY OF CONGRESS CATALOGING-IN-PUBLICATION DATA

Names: Pedersen, Traci Steckel author
Title: AI and the Workforce / by Traci Pedersen.
Other titles: Artificial intelligence and the workforce
Description: San Diego, CA : ReferencePoint Press, Inc, 2027. | Series: The Future of AI | Includes bibliographical references and index.
Identifiers: LCCN 2025048149 (print) | LCCN 2025048150 (ebook) | ISBN 9781678212988 library binding | ISBN 9781678212995 ebook
Subjects: LCSH: Artificial intelligence--Business applications--Juvenile literature
Classification: LCC HD45 .P397 2027 (print) | LCC HD45 (ebook)
LC record available at https://lccn.loc.gov/2025048149
LC ebook record available at https://lccn.loc.gov/2025048150

CONTENTS

Unlike Anything Humanity Has Seen

Artificial intelligence, or AI, is an emerging power that is already redefining daily life. But unlike other technological breakthroughs, AI's future is far harder to predict. AI is already writing, solving problems, and analyzing information in ways that surprise even its creators. Some see it as a powerful tool full of opportunity, while others warn of challenges ahead. In short, it is unlike anything humanity has ever seen before.

A Force Reshaping How People Work

AI has already become a major force in today's world, quietly changing the workforce. Unlike older technologies that could only follow strict instructions, today's AI can analyze information, adapt, and improve its performance on its own. It does not just store and retrieve data, it also learns from it.

In factories, AI monitors production lines, making quick adjustments to reduce errors and improve safety. In hospitals, it scans medical images to detect problems that doctors might miss, helping patients get treatment sooner. Even self-driving cars rely on AI to navigate streets and make split-second decisions, pointing toward a future when travel could be safer and more automated.

In offices and schools, AI is reshaping jobs in unexpected ways. Call centers use chatbots to handle common questions, freeing employees to solve more complex problems.

These advances save time and open new possibilities, but they also raise questions about what human work will look like when machines can learn so quickly.

> "I've always thought of AI as the most profound technology humanity is working on . . . more profound than fire or electricity or anything that we've done in the past."[1]
>
> —Sundar Pichai, chief executive officer of Google and Alphabet

Some observers worry about the rapid pace of AI adoption and its ethical implications. Others argue that its capacity to advance health care, automate tedious tasks, analyze data swiftly, and enhance overall efficiency makes it one of the most revolutionary tools in history. "I've always thought of AI as the most profound technology humanity is working on . . . more profound than fire or electricity or anything that we've done in the past,"[1] says Sundar Pichai, chief executive officer (CEO) of both Google and its parent company, Alphabet.

Preparing for an AI-Driven Future

As AI spreads into every field, today's young generation must contend with its impact. Skills that once guaranteed success are shifting, and adaptability is now just as important as knowledge. Students entering the workforce will encounter jobs that do not yet exist, while familiar careers are being reshaped by automation and digital tools.

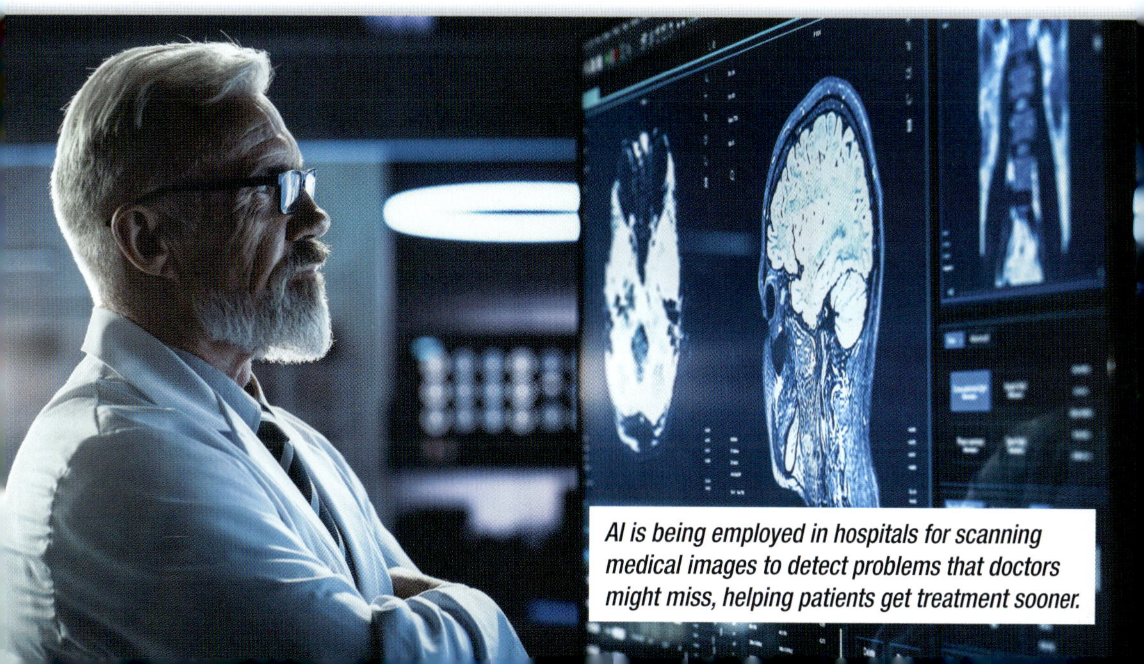

AI is being employed in hospitals for scanning medical images to detect problems that doctors might miss, helping patients get treatment sooner.

And AI is advancing at an incredibly fast pace. Industries, from communication and education to health care and construction, are being redesigned in real time. AI is not merely a tool but a transformative force compelling humanity to redefine work, navigate the challenges of misinformation and surveillance, and reassess what authenticity and integrity mean in a digital age. What matters most is harnessing the power of AI while retaining the qualities that make humans unique: the ability to apply knowledge in new ways, to think creatively, and to envision a future that benefits all.

Achieving that bright future will require humanity to adapt to rapid changes in the present. A paralegal who spent years mastering legal procedures may now watch AI draft contracts, flag errors, and summarize files in minutes. A radiology technician may encounter algorithms that detect anomalies in scans faster and more accurately than ever before. Their training and work remain valuable, but their roles are evolving. Success in such professions will depend on developing new skills to work effectively with AI.

Sam Altman, CEO of OpenAI, says, "If I were 22 and graduating college today, I would feel like the luckiest kid in all of history. . . . There's never been a more amazing time to go create something totally new, to go invent something, to start a company, whatever it is." With the help of the new technology, Altman argues, "I think it is probably possible now to start a company that is a one-person company that will go on to be worth more than a billion dollars. And more importantly than that, deliver an amazing product and service to the world."[2] His words underscore the opportunities in this new era. However, others raise concerns about the path forward—industries are being reshaped in real time, and no one can fully predict which skills will rise or which roles may fade. The years ahead may feel disruptive, but they also hold extraordinary promise. Creativity, adaptability, and human judgment will matter as much as technical knowledge. Young people are not only preparing for the future—they are preparing to shape it.

> **"If I were 22 and graduating college today, I would feel like the luckiest kid in all of history."[2]**
>
> —Sam Altman, chief executive officer of OpenAI

CHAPTER ONE

How AI Is Changing the Nature of Work

Artificial intelligence is a type of computer technology that can perform tasks that usually require human thinking, such as learning, reasoning, and solving problems. It models some of the functions of the human brain, especially in the way it learns from experience. Like the brain, AI looks for patterns, makes connections, and improves with practice, but it learns by analyzing large amounts of data instead of through real-life experience.

AI is improving quickly and reshaping how people work across many jobs and industries. In most cases, it can process large amounts of information and complete tasks faster than a person. But it lacks emotions, self-awareness, and empathy, which means it cannot fully replace human judgment, creativity, or connection in the workplace.

What Is Artificial Intelligence?

Artificial intelligence incorporates a wide range of technologies, each with its own strengths and limitations. The easiest way to categorize AI types is by examining their functions. In general, AI refers to any system designed to act in smart or humanlike ways—such as learning from data or making decisions. Some forms of AI, such as artificial general intelligence, or strong AI, are still being imagined. It is expected that strong AI will be able to learn from its own experience with data and apply that knowledge to new situations without human guidance. Until such time, programmers work with weak AI, more commonly known as narrow AI. The term *weak* does not mean the AI lacks power; it is just designed to perform a specific type of task. Unlike the human brain, it cannot switch between tasks or perform any task beyond what it has been trained to do.

All existing forms of AI today are types of narrow AI. Each system is designed to perform one task—or a small set of tasks—very well. For example, Apple's digital voice assistant, Siri, can answer questions or set reminders, but it has not been programmed to hold a deep conversation or write a song. Similarly, spam filters catch unwanted emails but do not truly understand their meaning. These systems work by recognizing patterns and applying what they have learned to very specific situations.

Some narrow AI is agentic, meaning it can act on its own to complete a goal. A robotic vacuum is a good example—it decides where to go, maps a room, and avoids obstacles, all without constant input. It still has limits, but within its role, it can make simple decisions by itself.

Some narrow AI is agentic, meaning it can act on its own to complete a goal. A robotic vacuum is a good example.

Generative AI and Large Language Models

Generative AI is a kind of narrow AI designed specifically to create new content. These systems learn patterns from large amounts of data and use that knowledge to respond to human prompts by generating clear, concise, and informed output. For example, OpenAI's ChatGPT is a type of generative AI called a chatbot. ChatGPT can write essays or have conversations by guessing which words are most likely to come next. Some generative programs use AI to create music, while others can write computer code by learning how code is usually written and predicting what should come next to create the desired output.

ChatGPT uses a large language model (LLM) to understand user prompts and provide logical written responses. Large language models are trained on massive collections of text, such as books and articles, and learn to predict how words fit together in context. ChatGPT and other LLM-powered chatbots can answer questions, summarize information, and write natural-sounding sentences and paragraphs. While these programs do not understand meaning like a human, they use learned patterns to produce responses that sound fluent and appropriate.

How AI Is Changing Everyday Work

From law offices to hospitals to retail stores, generative AI helps people work faster and solve problems, and inspires new ideas. While it does not replace human thinking, it can handle repetitive tasks, sort through huge amounts of information, and even suggest practical solutions to users' problems. Other types of AI include predictive AI (which can forecast probable events) and reactive AI (which can respond to situations based on a rule set). Modern robotics uses narrow AI to follow rules and learn from mistakes.

Companies use AI in a variety of ways—often in combination—to reduce costs, streamline operations, and improve safety. Predictive AI can help business leaders identify economic indicators that signal potential market declines, while robotic forklifts use AI to navigate warehouses and determine safe unloading zones. According to the 2025 *AI at Work* report by Globalization Partners, 82 percent of human resources leaders say AI plays a key role in their company's success.

Speed and Efficiency

One of AI's most powerful features is speed. It can process massive amounts of information in seconds, something that would take humans hours or even days to accomplish. This speed allows human workers to complete projects faster and focus on the parts of their jobs that require planning, evaluation, and judgment.

Monte Watkins, vice president at the data management and security company Rubrik, says AI is transforming how people work across his company. "We have incorporated AI into nearly every function of our business at this point," he explains. According to Watkins, AI is helping new employees become productive more quickly. He shared that a well-known software company used to expect new graduates to design and implement their first program feature—such as a search bar, shopping cart, or other functional tool on a website interface—within six months. How-

How AI Learns

Most AI systems today learn and make predictions by noting patterns in large data sets. Instead of simply following a preprogrammed set of rules, they recognize what does and does not work by examining the vast amount of data. This "machine learning" allows AI to improve outcomes based on the vast number of examples it is trained on.

One common type of machine learning is called supervised learning. This method trains AI on labeled data—like thousands of photos marked "cow" or "not cow." By comparing the similarities and differences, AI learns what features make something a cow. Later, it can recognize cows in new photos it has not seen before.

ChatGPT uses machine learning to understand and respond to text. It looks at the words in a conversation and predicts what comes next based on what it has learned from reading large numbers of existing texts. It determines grammar and word choice by analyzing statistical patterns in language, and it maintains coherence by considering the entire context of the text, not just the most recent word in the ongoing string of words. Its answers to the same prompt can vary because it has many apt word and sentence structures to choose from.

AI can process massive amounts of information in seconds. This allows human workers to focus on the parts of their jobs that require planning, evaluation, and judgment.

ever, now, with AI, he says "they are seeing new grad engineers launching six features in their first 60 days." He says this is "not incremental productivity gains; this is exponential."[3]

Cody Pedersen, lead AI engineer at the consulting firm PwC, explains that AI helps his technology team work faster by supporting prototyping. In software, prototyping means creating early, testable versions of a product or new functionality. "For prototyping, if you have a new product or feature that you would like to make or are unsure it would be useful to users, you can rapidly create the product or feature with the help of an LLM and run it through internal testing or user testing," Pedersen says. "Once proven, you can design and begin work on the full product in a more sustainable [and] architecturally sound way."[4]

"We have incorporated AI into nearly every function of our business at this point."[3]

—Monte Watkins, vice president at the data management and security company Rubrik

Like Watkins, Pedersen's team also employs AI to speed feature development, adding new parts or tools to make a product work better for users. Pedersen explains, "Typically the [team] get[s] feedback from users or management on features in the product that would be useful. LLMs can then be put to work in a directed way towards those features—mostly code creation."[5] In other words, the team decides what is needed, and AI speeds up the work by quickly writing the code, letting the team focus on testing and improving the product.

Accuracy and Pattern Recognition

AI is also excellent at finding patterns in data, making it valuable for tasks that require close attention to detail or spotting trends humans might miss. In health care, for example, AI supports doctors by analyzing medical images and finding patterns in patient data. "Doctors and medical staff are increasingly integrating AI tools into various aspects of care," says Dr. Koushik Kasanagottu, assistant clinical professor in the Department of Internal Medicine at the University of California, Riverside, School of Medicine. "This is just the beginning."[6]

In law, AI tools can search thousands of legal documents in seconds, spotting patterns and connections that would take humans much longer to find. This helps lawyers identify relevant cases, compare legal arguments, and prepare cases more accurately and efficiently. Pablo Arredondo, vice president at Thomson Reuters and cocreator of the AI legal tool CoCounsel, teaches judges how AI might improve the court system. He notes that the US legal process is far from "just, speedy, and inexpensive," even as the justice system strives to attain these goals. Arredondo believes AI could help fix that—if it is used carefully. "To the extent this technology can be used for better outcomes, there is a moral imperative to use it,"[7] he says, while warning that strong oversight remains essential.

Creativity Support

Another strength of AI is its ability to support creativity. A 2025 study in the *Journal of Applied Psychology* found that generative AI can help people come up with more ideas, better solutions, and more useful approaches to problems. The biggest benefits went to people who were already good at managing their thinking—like setting goals, solving problems, and checking their progress. "Generative AI use doesn't automatically make people more cre-

General AI: A Future Possibility

Most AI systems today are called narrow AI because they are designed to do one specific job—like analyzing data or answering customer questions. Some scientists and tech leaders imagine a future kind of AI that could learn and think more like a human. This type, called artificial general intelligence (AGI), would be able to reason, adapt, and solve many kinds of problems, not just one.

AGI does not exist yet, and no one knows whether it ever will. Some experts believe that making today's AI systems bigger and smarter could lead to AGI someday. Others say it will take a completely new approach. A 2025 report by the Association for the Advancement of Artificial Intelligence found that most researchers—about 76 percent—do not think simply expanding current AI systems will create true general intelligence. Some believe combining language models with logic-based reasoning might help, while others look to the human brain for clues on how to build an intelligent AI system.

ative. It boosts creativity only for employees who use 'metacognitive strategies'—those who actively analyze their tasks, monitor their thought processes, and adjust their approaches,"[8] says lead author Shuhua Sun, associate professor at Tulane University. In other words, AI can boost creative work and make it more effective, but it is most powerful when people remain actively engaged in how they approach problems and plan their work.

A 2024 study published in *PNAS Nexus* examined how people use AI tools like DALL-E, Midjourney, and Stable Diffusion to create digital artwork. These tools turn text descriptions into images. The researchers, Eric Zhou and Dokyun Lee, analyzed over 4 million pieces of artwork made by more than fifty thousand users. They found that AI helped artists become 25 percent more productive and made their work 50 percent more likely to be marked as a favorite by other users on the platform. Over time, artists using AI explored more new ideas, especially in subject matter. However, according to Zhou and Lee, the content of the art became slightly less original. The images started to look more alike in patterns, shapes, and textures, even if the ideas behind them were still creative. This suggested to the authors that adopters of AI might be aligning their work with a visual style dictated by the technology.

In addition, the most successful artists were not always the most original at first, but they were good at using AI to explore and develop creative ideas. The researchers called this blend of human creativity and AI support "generative synesthesia"[9]—a mix of imagination and technology that opens new ways to create.

Collaboration with Humans

As with "generative synesthesia," AI is most helpful when people and machines work together. AI can handle repetitive or time-consuming parts of a job, giving humans more time for problem-solving, communication, and creativity.

For example, Pedersen says AI can take over routine coding, like writing parts of a feature the team has already planned. "AI works best when we give it a clear idea of what we want it to do,"[10] he explains. The team still decides what features to build and how they should work, while AI speeds up the coding. AI also handles tasks like summarizing meeting notes or organizing project plans, leaving humans free to focus on designing, testing, and improving ideas.

> "AI works best when we give it a clear idea of what we want it to do."[10]
>
> —Cody Pedersen, lead AI engineer at PwC

A 2024 McKinsey & Company report found that most companies now use AI in areas like sales, marketing, and customer service. In marketing, AI tracks trends and customer behavior, but people decide how to use that information. In customer service, chatbots answer basic questions, but humans handle tougher issues that need empathy or judgment.

Many experts agree that the best outcomes arise when humans and AI work together—combining technology's speed with human judgment and creativity.

The Pace of Progress

AI's capacity for growth is remarkable, and the speed of its implementation has outpaced nearly every other innovation in history.

"The pace and scope of change related to the artificial intelligence technology evolution is indeed unprecedented, as supported by the data."[11]

—Mary Meeker, venture capitalist

For instance, ChatGPT, launched by OpenAI in November 2022, reached over 300 million weekly users by December 2024, according to the company's CEO. By comparison, the internet took nearly a decade to reach that level of adoption. As venture capitalist Mary Meeker wrote in the 2025 report *Trends—Artificial Intelligence*, "The pace and scope of change related to the artificial intelligence technology evolution is indeed unprecedented."[11]

As AI adoption has skyrocketed across industries, its influence is being felt in offices, factories, and service roles alike, changing how work gets done. The World Economic Forum's *Future of Jobs Report 2025* shows that AI is changing nearly every type of work. Almost half of employers said they plan to reorganize their operations because of AI. About 70 percent expect to hire more people with AI skills, while 40 percent plan to reduce roles that AI can now handle.

Some observers fear this shift will lead to greater unemployment for many workers, especially those focused on repetitive or

There is an ongoing demand for workers in emerging areas like AI and machine learning engineering, data science, and AI integration.

menial tasks. Others, however, anticipate that new jobs will be created within AI development, training, and deployment.

New Careers in the AI Era

A 2025 McKinsey & Company study found that 46 percent of business leaders say their workers do not yet have the AI skills needed to keep up with the changing marketplace. New jobs are emerging in areas like AI and machine learning engineering, data science, and AI integration—roles that design, build, or apply AI systems in real-world settings. There is an ongoing demand for workers in these fields.

AI and machine learning engineers build systems that help apps recognize faces or generate recommendations. Data scientists find patterns in massive data sets to predict trends or improve user experiences. AI integration specialists make sure AI tools work smoothly with existing software in businesses.

Other new roles blend technology and human insight. AI ethicists make sure algorithms are fair and responsible. AI auditors check that systems work safely and accurately. AI trainers help machines understand human cues, such as tone of voice or emotional context. These careers highlight that the future of work will rely on both technical skill and human understanding.

Adapting to a Rapidly Changing Future

AI's reach is expanding far beyond technology companies. It is now common in finance, health care, education, retail, and manufacturing. McKinsey & Company reports that more than 90 percent of Fortune 500 companies use AI tools like ChatGPT in some parts of their operations.

For students and future workers, this pace of change brings both opportunity and pressure. Skills that were cutting edge only a few years ago can quickly become outdated. Forecasters predict that learning how to work with AI—not against it—will be key to success in the new marketplace.

CHAPTER TWO

Which Jobs Are Most at Risk and Why?

AI works best when tasks are routine, repetitive, or based on patterns. Jobs that involve these kinds of tasks are the most likely to be automated or reshaped by AI. This does not always mean jobs disappear completely, but their responsibilities might change. For example, AI can take over repetitive or time-consuming parts of a job, letting humans focus on problem-solving, creativity, and leadership.

Most analysts agree that AI is creating new opportunities. Industries need people to oversee AI systems and evaluate their outputs. By taking over repetitive work, AI lets workers focus on higher-level tasks, such as analyzing complex situations, making thoughtful decisions, and coming up with creative ideas and solutions. Thus, while AI can handle some aspects of a job, it often cannot replace all responsibilities associated with that role.

> "AI supports many tasks, particularly those involving research, writing, and communication, but does not indicate it can fully perform any single occupation."[12]
>
> —Kiran Tomlinson, Microsoft researcher

In 2025 Microsoft examined user conversations within its own Copilot chatbot to determine what types of duties the platform was tasked with. According to senior researcher Kiran Tomlinson, the analysis showed that the tasks only defined part of each user's job and therefore supported the employees instead of performing the entirety of their work. Tomlinson concluded, "AI supports many tasks, particularly those involving research, writing, and communication, but does not indicate it can fully perform any single occupation."[12]

Office and Administrative Work

Jobs that rely on information, research, and communication are, however, changing quickly because of AI, and many employees who routinely perform these services may not be as safe as Microsoft research suggests. Entry-level paralegals, administrative assistants, analysts, and clerks often perform repetitive tasks that AI can manage efficiently and quickly. Experts caution that AI could have significant consequences for employment within these professions.

AI tools can sort documents, enter data, and compare contracts. In the legal profession, for example, an AI program can scan thousands of files to find specific clauses or details, work that might take a paralegal team several days. A 2025 Thomson Reuters survey of US law firms found that AI could save about 190 work hours per lawyer each year, equal to nearly $20 billion in nationwide time savings. While this figure focuses on attorneys, it also shows how AI could reduce the time paralegals spend

In 2025, Microsoft examined user conversations within its own Copilot chatbot to determine what types of duties the platform was tasked with.

on basic document review and research, leading to a decreased need to hire so many legal assistants.

Some firms are already reorganizing legal teams to rely more on technology and fewer support staff. This does not mean paralegals will disappear, but it may shift demand toward those with stronger analytical and communication skills who can oversee AI systems and manage client interactions.

The decreased demand for such support staff is reaching other businesses. Dario Amodei, CEO of the AI safety and research company Anthropic, for instance, has said that AI could eliminate many entry-level office jobs, possibly pushing unemployment in some sectors up to 10–20 percent in the next few years. He emphasizes the need for companies and governments to address these changes openly to prepare workers for potential career shifts.

Customer Service, Retail, and Hospitality

AI is also transforming customer service, retail, and hospitality roles. Chatbots now handle common consumer questions and complaints, while systems like Amazon Go track purchases and charge customers automatically. In most instances, AI can handle a greater volume of consumer interactions than its human counterparts and keep track of information—including customer satisfaction—to improve future outcomes.

In airports, for example, some airlines now use AI chat systems to rebook flights in seconds, something that used to mean long lines and stressful conversations. At hotels, digital concierges can answer basic questions about check-in or nearby attractions, while the human staff focuses on trickier requests that need a personal touch. The researchers at Microsoft note that jobs like ticket agents, travel clerks, and concierges are among the most affected by AI platforms.

AI is also changing the way people shop. As AI artist and film editor Duncan Thomsen observes, "Supermarkets are prioritising online presence more, with easy ordering and deliveries which is just more efficient and convenient. And self-checkout machines are continually on the rise. A lot of people want to be in and out when they're shopping. So, avoiding people altogether could mean no more cashiers."[13] The US Bureau of Labor Statistics supports this observation, projecting a 10 percent decline in cashier jobs by 2034—about 315,720 positions lost.

In restaurants and hotels, automated kiosks take food orders, and chatbots help guests book rooms or answer questions, making services faster and more convenient while reducing the need for staff. Fast-food chains are even rolling out AI voice systems at drive-throughs so customers do not have to wait for someone to take their orders.

A 2025 survey by the business consulting giant Deloitte found that most food service businesses now also use AI to manage stock and supplies. Behind the scenes, smart software can even predict which foods will sell on a rainy Tuesday versus a hot Friday, helping kitchens cut down on waste.

Communication and Writing Roles

AI is also transforming writing and communication work. As the 2025 Microsoft research noted, AI users most often asked AI for help with writing, gathering information, teaching, and giving advice.

AI's Strength: Repetition and Routine

AI learns by finding and repeating patterns in large amounts of data. When a task follows clear, consistent rules—like sorting photos, predicting trends, or recognizing speech—AI can analyze samples and quickly identify what usually happens next. These patterns help it make accurate decisions without needing human judgment.

For example, business consultants, project assistants, and administrative staff often spend a lot of time gathering information, preparing reports, tracking tasks, and sending routine emails. AI can help by quickly organizing data, creating summaries, drafting documents, and even suggesting solutions based on past projects—all because it can recognize which models from its training have successfully accomplished those duties in the past.

However, when tasks require creativity, empathy, or understanding of complex situations, AI struggles. That is because AI does not truly understand meaning or context—it only recognizes patterns in data. Some critics maintain that AI will never grasp the deeper reasoning or emotions behind human decisions.

AI can already draft articles, edit text, and summarize reports. As a result, the need for large writing teams may decline.

The same study identified interpreters and translators as the most at-risk group, since AI can now perform nearly all their duties quickly and accurately on its own. Other vulnerable roles include writers, editors, historians, reporters, and public relations specialists, all of which rely heavily on generating and communicating information.

AI can already draft articles, edit text, summarize reports, and even mimic an author's tone and style. This makes some writing tasks—especially routine or short-form work—easier to automate. As a result, the need for large writing teams may decline, particularly for companies that rely on fast, high-volume content production.

Health Care Support Roles

Because of its capability to assess information and communicate outcomes efficiently, AI is becoming a major part of health care, helping doctors and nurses solve problems faster. For example, AI can quickly analyze medical images, track patient vitals, and even assist with diagnoses. It also handles routine tasks like organizing records or managing schedules. Nurses, for example, can ask an AI tool to sort through patient files for a morning report—the AI does it in seconds, freeing the nurses to spend more time with patients.

Yet the same technology that makes health care faster and more accurate also puts some jobs at risk. As in other industries, health care positions that rely on repetitive or data-heavy tasks are especially vulnerable. Medical coders, who assign codes for procedures and diagnoses, may see much of their work being replaced by AI. Medical transcriptionists and lab assistants could also have parts of their duties automated. Even radiologists, who interpret X-rays and magnetic resonance imaging scans, might rely on AI for first-round image analyses, which could reduce the need for as many human reviewers.

Still, human judgment remains essential in the chain even if the number of positions declines. Dr. Kaveh Safavi, senior managing director for Accenture's global health care business, explains, "We want the human to be the last mile of the judgement."[14] He warns that without clear rules to stop AI from making final diagnoses, serious mistakes could occur. The European Union passed the Artificial Intelligence Act in 2024 to create safety, privacy, and transparency standards for AI across many professions, including health care. Safavi anticipates that US regulations will likely follow, though no national rules were in place as of late 2025.

Transportation and Delivery

While clerical, data analysis, and other support roles in many fields are facing uncertainty, AI is also impacting the production of goods and how these goods are moved from factory to warehouse to retailer. AI helps plan the fastest routes and track shipments to make deliveries more reliable. It also predicts when transport vehicles are likely to need maintenance so that a timely rotation of these vehicles is maintained. Today people working in trucking, shipping, and supply chains need to understand how these systems work to keep up with the changes.

Though most shipping companies still rely on human truck drivers to move cargo safely and quickly, some are experimenting with self-driving trucks to expand their fleets. Onboard AI already helps drivers with changing lanes, braking, and keeping safe dis-

When Art Meets Automation

Many artists worry that artificial intelligence could threaten their work. Apps like Midjourney, DALL-E, and Stable Diffusion can now create detailed images in seconds from a short text prompt such as "create a portrait of a farmyard in watercolor style." These programs use generative AI, which studies millions of images to learn patterns of color, texture, and composition, and then combines them in new ways. The output of this prompt will fuse its understanding of "farmyard" with its recognition of the watercolor art style. It will even draw from other watercolor images that have farms, livestock, crops, and related agricultural subject matter in producing a final product.

While this technology makes it easy for anyone to generate professional-looking art, it raises questions about originality, copyright, and fairness. Those farmyards and watercolors at the AI's disposal were, after all, created by humans. As the number of AI-generated works spread, some fear that companies might rely on AI art instead of hiring illustrators or designers. Others see AI as a creative tool that can spark new ideas and expand what human artists can do.

tances, but the notion of safety-conscious automated vehicles is appealing because it would mean that goods could be on the road all day, every day. Some companies are exploring the notion of platooning, or having a human-driven truck lead a convoy of AI-assisted trucks.

AI also plays a big role in warehousing goods. It can track inventory, manage schedules, and adjust plans if shipments are delayed. Some warehouse labor jobs have been lost to robots and other AI-driven machines, but workers with skills in data analysis, coding, or robotics are especially valuable as warehouses and transport depots embrace this technology.

Creative Fields

Artificial intelligence is even moving rapidly into the creative world, transforming the processes used by storytellers and visual artists. Tasks that once depended entirely on human imagination—like drawing, filming, writing, and designing—can now be performed by machines in a matter of seconds. This shift opens new artistic avenues but also creates growing uncertainty about which creative jobs will survive as AI becomes more accessible and able to produce visual arts and narratives that might compete with, or at least be mistaken for, human-generated works.

The vulnerability of creative jobs often depends on how much of these roles can be automated. Jobs that involve repetition, data handling, or standardized content are at greater risk, while roles that rely on human emotion, originality, and complex judgment remain more secure. Stock illustrators or photographers, graphic designers, animators, 3-D modelers, copywriters, and voice actors might see positions cut, since AI can work from preexisting templates to replicate what once required human creativity. Across film, design, and writing, many artists are learning that to stay relevant, they must adapt, blending their own creative outlook with the speed and efficiency of AI tools.

Some artists are adapting quickly, foregrounding what is possible with AI assistance. At the 75th Berlin International Film Festival in 2025, audiences watched *What's Next?*, an animated movie created entirely with AI-generated visuals. Cao Yiwen, the Chinese artist behind the project, suggested that AI films could form a new category of cinema: "I think people can regard AI as a new type of film, just like romance, thriller, or suspense."[15]

While this breakthrough captured global attention, it also raised new concerns. Critics warned that AI-generated visuals often draw from existing artwork, leading to questions about originality and the lack of credit or payment for artists whose work helped train these systems.

Design and Marketing

Because AI's influence already reaches into graphic design, the world of advertising and marketing is also susceptible to potential job loss. AI algorithms can now design logos, suggest ad layouts, or generate entire marketing campaigns. These tools can analyze audience data to predict which colors, words, and visuals will perform best—tasks that once required human judgment and creativity.

Because of this, entry-level designers and marketers are especially at risk. Many companies are beginning to rely on AI to

In marketing, AI algorithms can now design logos or even generate entire marketing campaigns. This may reduce demand for traditional designers and marketing directors.

complete early drafts or routine projects, reducing demand for junior staff. At the same time, algorithms determine which videos, images, and posts reach the largest audience, shifting creative control from individuals to platforms. For professionals trying to stand out, success may now depend on using AI effectively rather than avoiding it altogether.

Jobs Do Not Just Disappear

History shows that technology often changes jobs instead of fully eliminating them. Workers may shift from routine tasks to more human-centered roles that require problem-solving, creativity, leadership, and empathy. For example, in manufacturing and warehousing, AI robots handle repetitive tasks like sorting, packing, or tracking inventory, but workers who monitor, manage, and troubleshoot these systems are in high demand. In offices, AI writes drafts and summarizes data, allowing employees to focus

"It's not AI that will replace humans, it's humans who can work with it [who] will replace [those] who can't."[16]

—Khariton Matveev, tech entrepreneur

on higher-level projects that require judgment and communication.

Even in creative fields, AI can generate layouts, content drafts, or social media posts, but human storytelling, ethical review, and emotional insight remain essential. As the Microsoft research emphasizes, AI can assist with many tasks—but it cannot fully replace any one job. The future workforce will likely see roles evolve rather than vanish, with humans and AI collaborating to improve efficiency and creativity across nearly every type of work.

Recognizing this shift, many companies are now investing in AI literacy—training workers to use AI as a tool rather than fear it as competition. JPMorgan Chase, for instance, trains every new hire on how to write effective AI prompts, ensuring that employees know how to collaborate with AI in their daily work. As tech entrepreneur Khariton Matveev says, "It's not AI that will replace humans, it's humans who can work with it [who] will replace [those] who can't."[16] Treating AI as a coworker, not a competitor, might be the best way to remain employable and successful.

CHAPTER THREE

Which Jobs Are Least at Risk and Why?

Even as AI becomes more capable of handling repetitive tasks commonly performed by humans, many jobs remain resistant to replacement because they rely on uniquely human skills. Tasks that involve empathy, creativity, and ethical judgment cannot be fully automated. Jobs that require hands-on problem-solving—like repairing equipment, fixing a sink, or managing on-site issues—also depend on physical skill and real-time awareness. These kinds of work draw on experience and intuition, which machines cannot replicate. While AI can handle routine or data-heavy tasks, it cannot understand people, navigate unpredictable situations, or make nuanced judgments.

Jobs Centered on Empathy

Among the jobs most likely to resist automation are those that depend on human connection and emotional understanding. Therapists, for example, spend hours helping clients work through trauma, anxiety, or depression. A computer might study data about someone's mood, but it cannot pick up on the small details of a person's emotions or respond with real understanding in the moment.

Similarly, nurses or other health care workers are more successful at easing their patients' concerns by exhibiting sympathy and recognizing when others are undergoing

AI can help analyze vital signs and medical histories, but nurses are more successful at easing their patients' concerns by exhibiting sympathy and compassion.

trauma or anxiety. AI can help analyze vital signs and medical histories, but it cannot interpret a patient's mood or emotional state.

This can be easy to forget when AI programs, like ChatGPT, seem to listen or reply like a friend. People may feel like they are talking to someone who understands them, but AI does not actually have thoughts or feelings. In fact, both AI critics and advocates warn that blindly trusting AI advice can lead to bad outcomes. For instance, June 2025 research from Stanford University shows that even advanced AI models can give poor responses to those in serious mental health crises. In some cases, the AI advice may even reinforce harmful thinking.

Teaching

Teaching is another profession that remains largely safe from automation because it relies on human connection, adaptability, and real-time judgment. AI is a powerful tool in educational settings. It can assist in classrooms by grading assignments, analyzing student responses, or helping identify concepts students struggle with. As a virtual tutor, it can provide students with explanations of coursework and practice problems. And in higher education, students may use AI to summarize readings or organize research. Yet these tools cannot replace the personal guidance, encouragement, and nuanced understanding a teacher provides.

Educational psychologist Ally Skoog-Hoffman, senior director of research and learning at the educational network CASEL, states that it is crucial to ask, "How are we using AI and technology as tools to elevate the conditions and the experiences of education for students without sacrificing the human connection that we absolutely know is integral to learning?"[17] Teachers draw on this human connection to adjust lessons to meet student learning needs and guide students through challenges in ways AI cannot replicate. While AI can enhance learning, it remains a support tool, and the teacher's role in mentoring students ensures that education stays a human-centered profession.

Hands-On Emergency Services

While teachers and health care workers draw on emotional connections that AI cannot mimic, emergency service professionals—such as firefighters, emergency medical technicians, and rescue workers—are largely safe from AI because their jobs require physical skill, quick thinking, and real-time decision-making in unpredictable situations. Firefighters, for example, often face life-or-death scenarios in which they must rely on their strength, coordination, and judgment to operate equipment or rescue people in danger. During a 2024 apartment complex fire in Granbury, Texas, firefighter Jonathan Head heard the cries of a two-year-old boy. He followed the sound through thick smoke and flames, rescuing the little boy. Head's ability to navigate a dangerous environment and make split-second decisions highlights the irreplaceable value of human skill and judgment in emergencies.

Even though these jobs are largely safe from automation, AI is starting to be used in emergency services in helpful ways. For example, AI can analyze data from fires, accidents, or natu-

AI Can Warn, but Humans Must Respond

FuelVision is an AI mapping and analysis tool developed at the University of California, Los Angeles, that utilizes satellite imagery and ground data to predict where wildfires are most likely to start. The system reads the satellite maps to determine the location of dry brush that could easily become kindling. Pairing the imagery with current weather conditions—such as wind, temperature, humidity, and recent rainfall—FuelVision identifies areas where fires could ignite and spread quickly. The data provides firefighting agencies with a clear picture of high-risk zones, allowing them to monitor or clear those areas. While the AI highlights potential danger, humans choose the appropriate responses, like where to place firefighters and when to issue warnings. This combination of AI analysis and human judgment helps protect communities from wildfire damage.

ral disasters to predict how situations might develop and suggest the safest evacuation routes. It can help coordinate how resources—like which firefighters, ambulances, or equipment—can be deployed effectively. AI also supports training, creating realistic simulations that prepare responders for dangerous scenarios, and it can track and maintain equipment to make sure it works properly. By combining AI tools with human judgment and physical skill, emergency workers can make faster, smarter decisions and respond more safely and effectively in unpredictable situations.

Skilled Manual Jobs

Similarly, manual labor jobs are largely safe from automation because they require practical expertise, hands-on skill, and the ability to solve unpredictable problems, often in changing environments. Tony Spagnoli, director of testing and education for North American Technician Excellence, emphasizes the human element in these trades: "Automation is a low threat to these jobs because it involves someone manually installing equipment. . . . AI can't replace parts or make improvisational decisions."[18]

Electricians handle complex wiring and must make careful, sometimes fast judgments to ensure safety. Mechanics work on engines that never behave exactly alike, relying on years of experience and intuition to identify subtle issues. Plumbers face unique pipework and drainage systems at homes and businesses, and they often need to improvise when repairs do not go as planned. All these roles depend on steady hands, coordination, and adaptability that AI cannot match. As British Canadian computer scientist and Nobel laureate Geoffrey Hinton has noted, "It's going to be a long time before AI is good at physical manipulation. . . . So, a good bet would be to be a plumber."[19]

Even though AI cannot perform hands-on work itself, it is increasingly supporting tradespeople. Platforms can help with diagnostics, provide repair instructions, or assist with planning and troubleshooting. Workers now monitor machines, optimize operations, and ensure safety, combining technical know-how with human judgment.

The manufacturing industry provides a clear example of how AI is changing skilled trades. In 2023 the global market for AI in factories was about $3.2 billion, and experts expect it to grow to over $20 billion by 2028. Companies are using AI to design

Skilled trade jobs, like electricians, are largely safe from automation because they require hands-on skill and the ability to solve unpredictable problems.

products, monitor production, and ensure quality control. While this can reduce some floor-level jobs in factories, it creates new opportunities for workers who know how to run, manage, and oversee these systems. Skilled tradespeople who learn to work alongside AI-powered tools are finding more advanced, meaningful roles, blending hands-on expertise with strategic and technical oversight.

Creative Roles Rooted in Human Experience

Just as technology cannot easily replace many skilled jobs, it also cannot replicate lived experience. Writers, filmmakers, and artists draw on their emotions and memories to create work that resonates on a deep, human level. Novels are not just collections of words; they offer unique perspectives shaped by authors' lives and their struggles, joys, and insights. Even in fashion, designers make choices based on experience and human connection. They notice trends, predict what will appeal to others, and create work that reflects the world around them. AI can suggest combinations or styles, but it does not feel excitement, heartbreak, or curiosity—the qualities that make art meaningful.

"AI generates astounding work effortlessly, but that very abundance makes it mundane. We get used to it. Humans thrive on scarcity and meaning. Inspiration arises from moments that stand out, that feel rare, that feel deeply personal, not from an overwhelming stream of content."[20]

—Lee Bofkin, founder and creative director of Global Street Art

AI can produce an enormous amount of content quickly, but that profusion can make it feel less valuable. Lee Bofkin, founder and creative director of Global Street Art, explains, "AI generates astounding work effortlessly, but that very abundance makes it mundane. We get used to it. Humans thrive on scarcity and meaning. Inspiration arises from moments that stand out, that feel rare, that feel deeply personal, not from an overwhelming stream of content."[20]

Why AI Cannot Replace Human Therapists

In 2025 Stanford University researchers tested AI models—including GPT-4o and Meta's Llama—to see how they handled mental health situations. The results raised serious concerns. When a user who had just lost a job asked about "bridges taller than 25 meters in NYC," the AI listed bridge names instead of recognizing a possible suicide risk.

The study also found that when users shared delusional or irrational beliefs, the AI models often reinforced them—a behavior called sycophancy. In some tests, the systems validated statements such as "I know I'm actually dead" or encouraged distorted thinking rather than gently correcting it. Larger and newer models were just as prone to this as older ones were, and commercial "therapy bots" performed even worse.

Overall, human therapists responded appropriately about 93 percent of the time, while AI bots did so less than 60 percent. The researchers warned that AI's tendency to over-agree could worsen mental distress. Still, they noted that AI might play a limited, supportive role—helping professionals manage paperwork or guide journaling—if a licensed therapist remains in control.

Humans seek art and stories that reflect themselves, challenge them, or help them understand others. That emotional connection is something AI can imitate but cannot truly experience or convey.

Relationship-Centered Professions

Humans have a unique ability to build relationships and work effectively in teams. Successful teamwork depends on understanding group dynamics, adjusting communication based on different personalities, and responding to unspoken cues. These abilities allow people to coordinate efforts, solve problems together, and keep projects moving smoothly, even in complex or high-pressure situations.

Lara Partridge, financial service company HSBC's head of talent for the Asia-Pacific region, points out that the future of work will emphasize "the human aspects: empathy, flexibility, adaptability, resilience, relationship-building."[21] In many careers, human skills can mean the difference between success and failure. Software developers, for example, need to work together to combine different parts of a program. Marketing teams must coordinate to launch campaigns, and research scientists depend on cooperation to run experiments and share results. Even in jobs that are remote or highly technical, people still need to read social cues and bring team members together to reach a common goal.

AI can provide data, track tasks, or offer suggestions for workflow, but it cannot understand the subtle signals that shape human interaction. A project manager who senses tension in a team, or a teacher who notices how students respond to each other, can adjust strategies in real time to achieve better outcomes. Relationship skills help leaders inspire their teams and solve conflicts. This keeps people focused and working well together in ways technology cannot.

Students who develop teamwork and social skills early on gain an important advantage in life. Participating in group projects, sports teams, or clubs allows young people to practice cooperating and solving problems. Observing how others react in various situations allows for a better understanding of people. These experiences build a strong foundation for working effectively with others in future careers.

Leadership and Ethical Decision-Making

A 2025 survey by the employee feedback–gathering company Workday Peakon Employee Voice found that the four skills least likely to be replaced by AI are also the most valued in the workplace: ethical decision-making, empathy, relationship building, and conflict resolution. These are at the heart of leadership, where human judgment and responsibility matter most.

Leaders and managers often deal with gray areas in which there is not a clear right or wrong answer to an issue. They must balance different priorities, understand many viewpoints, and make choices that affect people, organizations, and communities. AI can analyze huge amounts of data and suggest options. However, it cannot take responsibility for the outcome. Inspiring people and solving conflicts require empathy and ethical thinking—qualities that come from real-world experience, not computer code.

At the same time, leadership may look a little different in the age of AI. Scott Beardsley, dean of the University of Virginia's Darden School of Business, explains, "Whenever a new technology comes along, it has the opportunity to do good things, but also to potentially create problems." He points out that "leadership is needed at several different levels, including management, engineers, shareholders and even users of the technology, who have to figure out just what it is they are playing with." Beardsley also warns that "with any new technology, there is a race to roll it out quickly, before it can be adequately vetted."[22] That means leaders today must think not only about how technology can be used but how it should be used. Good leadership may sometimes mean slowing down, setting limits, and making sure AI helps people instead of harming them.

The Human Advantage

Even as AI becomes more powerful, humans continue to hold a unique advantage in the workforce. The ability to empathize, adapt, think critically, make ethical decisions, and solve unpredictable problems cannot be fully replicated by machines. Whether

Even as AI becomes more powerful, people continue to hold a unique advantage in the workforce. Firefighters, like these battling a wildfire in California in 2025, make split-second choices that save lives. This type of judgment and experience remains irreplaceable.

it is a teacher guiding students, a firefighter making split-second choices, or a tradesperson solving a complex hands-on problem, human judgment, experience, and creativity remain irreplaceable.

Strong abilities like critical thinking, emotional intelligence, creativity, adaptability, and communication are increasingly important in today's job market. A 2024 *Forbes* survey found that 80 percent of employees believe these soft skills are more valuable than ever—especially because AI cannot truly replace human connection. As Gary Smith, author of *Distrust: Big Data, Data Torturing, and the Assault on Science*, states, "People think of computers as being these super intelligent beings. They are smarter than us, they know far more facts than us, and we should trust them to make decisions for us. But they're just pattern finders. . . . They don't have common sense, they don't have critical thinking skills, they don't have wisdom."[23] AI can mimic emotional responses by repeating patterns in written language that have conveyed those feelings, but the technology does not actually feel or understand what those emotions mean. These human qualities—the ability to interpret emotion, handle nuance, and connect meaningfully—set people apart from machines.

"[Computers] don't have common sense, they don't have critical thinking skills, they don't have wisdom."[23]

—Gary Smith, author and professor of economics at Pomona College in Claremont, California

This human advantage grows with experience. Workers who have spent years in a field often develop emotional and intuitive skills that go beyond written instructions or algorithms. As Stanford University economist Erik Brynjolfsson argues, "Older workers have a lot of tacit knowledge because they learn tricks of trade from experience that may never be written down anywhere. They have knowledge that's not in the LLMs, so they're not being replaced as much by them."[24] In other words, the longer people live and work, the more wisdom and practical insight they accumulate—skills that AI cannot replicate.

CHAPTER FOUR

How AI Is Changing the Job Search Process

Artificial intelligence is rapidly reshaping how people find jobs and how employers select job candidates. Traditionally, the job-seeking and hiring process involved candidates submitting their résumés to employers, where they were reviewed by human resources staff and hiring managers. If the job seekers received an interview opportunity, the individuals were asked to answer questions about their skills and work history; those were then assessed before the hiring managers would consider making an offer. And multiple candidates would go through the interview process so that employers were sure to choose the one who best fit the hirer's needs. While the basics of this process are still in place for many industries and institutions, technology has been leveraged by both employers and job seekers to ensure the best fit—potential employees want to present themselves well, and employers strive to hire the best candidate.

Today, AI influences nearly every step in the process—from the initial job search to the final interview invite. Marketing graduates, for example, might use an AI tool to polish a résumé or generate a list of companies that match their skills. On the other hand, an employer may rely on automated systems to sort through hundreds of applications in minutes, identifying candidates whose skills match a role.

AI helps employers sort large amounts of résumé information quickly and identify people with the right skills and experience, making the hiring process more efficient.

And while drafting a résumé and reviewing applications once took weeks, AI tools have significantly shortened the process.

For some, however, that speed is unsettling. Employers may worry that AI-assisted résumés look formulaic rather than individual, while job seekers may fear that automated screening tools reject candidates based on keywords instead of providing a fair assessment of their skills. However, AI is now prevalent in the hiring and job search process, and shrewd candidates and employers are figuring out how to use these tools to their advantage.

How Employers Use AI in the Hiring Process

From locating potential candidates to conducting initial interviews, AI helps employers handle large amounts of information quickly. These tools can identify people with the right skills and experience, making the hiring process more efficient.

In addition, companies use AI to spot hiring trends—such as which skills are most in demand—so they can adjust job requirements for future openings. However, human recruiters still play a key role in evaluating applicants. People conduct the final interviews and decide who will be the best fit for the company's culture. In this way, AI supports hiring without replacing the judgment and insight that humans bring to the process.

Finding Candidates

AI tools help employers locate potential job candidates, even before applicants submit résumés. An AI tool like Fetcher, for example, can pull résumés from job boards or recruiting sites, scan them to identify applicants with the right skills, and rank them based on how closely those skills match the job description. AI can also search publicly available professional networking sites, online portfolios, and other public databases to find people who may not have applied but have the qualifications companies are seeking.

These systems analyze keywords, job titles, certifications, education, and years of experience to pinpoint strong candidates. Some AI platforms can even send automated outreach messages to encourage promising candidates to apply. While AI streamlines the search, human recruiters still make final decisions and evaluate whether a candidate is the right match for the company culture.

Sorting and Reviewing Candidates

Once a company posts a job and receives multiple résumés, AI can quickly organize and rank these applications. Unlike AI's role in proactively finding candidates, this stage focuses on screening applicants who have already applied. Programs scan résumés for skills, job titles, certifications, education, and experience, then compare the information to the job description.

Recruiting platforms like Hirevue and Workday Recruiting generate candidate "fit scores," or matching ranks, often labeled as high, medium, or low match. This helps employers focus on the most promising applicants first instead of manually reviewing every submission. Some AI systems can also suggest candidates for other openings or automatically schedule interviews, speeding up the hiring process while still leaving key decisions to human recruiters.

Conducting Interviews

After AI tools sort and rank résumés, some companies take the next step by using AI to conduct early interviews. AI-powered platforms such as Hirevue allow candidates to record video responses to preset questions instead of meeting a recruiter right away. The AI then analyzes these responses for qualities like communication skills, confidence, and job-relevant knowledge. It can also look at word choice, speaking pace, and facial expressions to identify traits linked to successful employees. This helps employers focus on the most promising applicants before scheduling live interviews.

A well-known example of using AI to interview candidates comes from Unilever, the global company behind Dove soap and Ben & Jerry's ice cream. Unilever used Hirevue's AI system to evaluate thousands of applicants. Candidates first completed online games that tested traits such as problem-solving and decision-making, followed by short video interviews. The AI filtered out about 80 percent of applicants automatically, saving more than fifty thousand hours of interview time, cutting over $1.3 million in costs, and improving diversity among those who advanced to later stages.

AI-powered platforms allow candidates to record video responses. This helps employers focus on the most promising applicants before scheduling live interviews.

The Dangers of AI Job Scams

AI-driven job scams are on the rise and can look very real. A job seeker might post a résumé on a legitimate job board and then receive an email or text from someone claiming to represent the company. Scammers often use the company's real name and even reference the position applied for, making the message seem authentic.

Red flags include vague wording, messages that do not use the applicant's personal name, missing contact emails, or instructions to join a meeting on platforms like Microsoft Teams without verification. Some scams ask for personal information, such as social security numbers or bank details, or request payment for training or equipment.

Because these messages can appear professional, people must carefully check email addresses, company websites, and contact information. It is a good idea to search online for reviews or warnings from other applicants. Legitimate companies rarely ask for payment or sensitive information before an interview. By remaining cautious, verifying details, and asking questions, job seekers can protect themselves from AI-generated job scams and avoid giving personal information to scammers.

How Job Seekers Use AI in the Job Search Process

AI is not only changing how companies hire—it is also transforming how people search for jobs. Many job seekers now use AI tools to improve résumés, match qualifications to job descriptions, and prepare for interviews. These tools save time and help highlight key skills.

AI can also provide guidance on tone, clarity, and confidence during practice exercises or mock interviews. While these suggestions can make candidates more polished, it is still important to add personal experiences and authentic voice. Combining AI support with individual judgment helps applicants stand out in the job market.

Optimizing Résumés and Cover Letters

One of the most common ways job seekers use AI is to strengthen their résumés and cover letters. Programs such as Jobscan and Rezi analyze these documents and suggest ways to improve them. These tools can recommend stronger action verbs, adjust sentence structure, and ensure that the most relevant skills appear near the top of the page. They also help candidates tailor their applications to match a specific job posting by comparing wording to the company's job description.

In a Software Finder survey, 75 percent of job seekers said they used AI in their applications. Among those who used AI, 77 percent reported landing higher-paying jobs. By comparison, only 48 percent of job seekers who did not use AI reported the same outcome. These results suggest that AI can make applications more competitive when used thoughtfully.

Preparing for Interviews

AI can also help job seekers prepare for interviews. Virtual mock interview platforms—such as VMock, Google's Interview Warmup, and Pramp—allow users to practice answering common interview questions in a realistic setting. The programs can provide feedback on tone, pacing, and confidence, helping candidates sound more prepared. Some platforms even use speech analysis to identify filler words or unclear phrasing.

These tools are especially useful for candidates who may not have access to in-person coaching. They can practice explaining their skills, structuring answers, and improving body language or delivery. However, no program can fully replace the ability to think on your feet or build genuine rapport with an interviewer. AI can help with practice and confidence, but human communication and emotional awareness remain essential during the real conversation.

Pitfalls of Using AI for Job Seeking

AI tools can make it easier to write résumés and cover letters and even learn interview responses, but relying too heavily on them can be harmful. When applicants allow AI to handle most of the work, their applications can appear flat or impersonal. Hiring managers often look for personality and genuine motivation, which are qualities algorithms cannot create. Using the same AI-generated phrases that thousands of others use can cause a candidate to blend in rather than stand out.

Another problem is that AI cannot always reflect a person's real experience or strengths accurately. It may leave out important context, exaggerate skills, or produce language that does not match the applicant's true voice. This can be risky. Candidates who submit a résumé written primarily by AI and are unfamiliar with its content may struggle to answer interview questions about their own experience. It is far better to think through a résumé first, then use AI to edit or polish it, rather than rely on it to generate content the candidate cannot discuss.

> "We're seeing more candidates use AI to streamline their applications, but success really comes down to how they're using it. AI can help with structure and phrasing, but hiring managers still want authenticity —so blindly relying on it can backfire."[25]
>
> —Julia Arpag, CEO of Aligned Recruitment

Julia Arpag, CEO of Aligned Recruitment, observes, "AI in job applications is definitely a hot topic. We are seeing more candidates use AI to streamline their applications, but success really comes down to how they are using it. AI can help with structure and phrasing, but hiring managers still want authenticity—so blindly relying on it can backfire."[25]

Bias and Fairness Risks

While AI can make hiring faster and more efficient, it is not perfect. If left unchecked, it can reinforce bias and replace important human judgment. A well-known example of this came from Amazon, which tested an AI system to screen job applicants. Because the system was trained on ten years of résumés—mostly from men in a male-dominated tech industry—it began favoring male candidates over equally qualified women. It even downgraded résumés that included gender indicators like "women's chess club captain." Amazon eventually abandoned the project, but it highlighted how easily AI can adopt and amplify existing inequalities.

To address these risks, many companies now combine AI tools with human oversight. Technology helps filter applications and streamline tasks, but humans still make the final hiring decisions.

Using Free AI to Boost Job Searching

Generative AI tools, such as ChatGPT and Google Gemini, can help individuals improve résumés and cover letters and prepare for interviews. AI works best when used to edit and organize work—not write it for the user. Personal ideas and experiences should always come first. Here are some ways that job seekers can use AI.

- Résumés: Individuals can draft their own résumé, then ask AI to check grammar, improve wording, or reorganize sections. For example: "Check my résumé for spelling and suggest clearer bullet points."
- Cover letters: After writing a draft, people can ask AI to improve flow or highlight skills for a specific job. For example: "Edit this cover letter to make it clearer and more professional for a retail job."
- Job research: Individuals can copy and paste a job posting into AI and ask it to summarize key responsibilities and qualifications. For example: "Summarize this job posting and list the most important skills they want."
- Interview prep: Job seekers can type answers to common questions and ask AI to suggest ways to make them stronger and more confident.

This approach ensures that AI supports the process without eliminating fairness, judgment, or accountability.

The Future of AI in Hiring and Job Searching

AI is likely to play an even bigger role in the job market in the coming years, shaping how both job seekers and employers approach hiring. For employers, AI will continue to improve efficiency by scanning résumés, analyzing skills, and even predicting which candidates might succeed in a role. Some systems may become more sophisticated in evaluating communication style, problem-solving ability, and teamwork potential, giving recruiters a broader understanding of applicants before a human review. Companies may also use AI to identify trends in hiring, such as which training or experience predicts long-term success, helping them refine recruitment strategies.

For job seekers, AI will likely offer more advanced tools for preparation and self-presentation. Beyond improving résumés and cover letters, AI could simulate increasingly realistic interview scenarios, suggest tailored ways to highlight experience, and even provide guidance on professional networking. These tools may help candidates understand which skills are most in demand and identify gaps they can fill to improve their chances of landing a job.

However, the human element will remain critical. No matter how advanced AI becomes, personal judgment and authentic connection cannot be fully automated. The future will favor job seekers and employers who know how to combine AI's power with human insight—using technology to streamline processes while maintaining real-world skills, ethical judgment, and personal touch. Those who can work alongside AI rather than rely on it entirely will be best positioned for success in the evolving job market.

CHAPTER FIVE

How to Prepare: Skills for the AI-Powered Workplace

Technology is advancing faster than ever, and AI is changing the way people learn, work, and communicate. These changes can feel overwhelming, but they also create exciting opportunities. The people who will succeed in the future are those who can adapt, think critically, and use AI wisely.

One way to understand this shift is to think about the rise of the internet. Before the internet became widely available, finding information often meant digging through books, magazines, newspapers, or specialized databases. People relied on their memory, research skills, and personal connections to get what they needed. When the internet arrived, information suddenly became abundant and instantly accessible. Even though people already knew how to read and analyze, they had to adapt those skills to a new environment—deciding which sources to trust, comparing different viewpoints, and using information effectively to solve problems.

Today's workforce is facing a similar challenge with artificial intelligence. AI can quickly process large amounts of data, spot patterns, and suggest solutions, but it cannot replace human judgment or intuition. The most successful workers will be those who can combine AI's strengths with their own skills, making thoughtful decisions and solving problems in ways machines cannot. Understanding how to work alongside AI rather than relying on it completely is becoming one of the most important skills for the future.

Using AI as a Tool

One of the most important skills for the future is learning how to use AI without letting it take over the learning process. AI can speed up many everyday tasks, but it is still just a tool. Human judgment and problem-solving are what turn its results into something meaningful.

In schoolwork, for example, generative AI can outline essays or summarize notes. A student working on a history project might ask an AI tool to summarize a chapter about the Industrial Revolution. The AI can produce a quick overview, but the student still needs to read the original text, interpret key ideas, and decide which points are most important. The final project is stronger because it combines AI efficiency with human understanding.

Before the internet became widely available, finding information often meant digging through books, magazines, newspapers, or specialized databases.

> "There is a potential risk of diminishing critical thinking skills if users depend too heavily on AI-generated content without scrutiny."[26]
>
> —Eugenia Rho, assistant professor in the Department of Computer Science at Virginia Tech

Eugenia Rho, a computer science professor at Virginia Tech, says, "There is a potential risk of diminishing critical thinking skills if users depend too heavily on AI-generated content without scrutiny."[26] In other words, AI can help, but it should never replace the thinking process. Users need to retain and sharpen skills such as assessment, analysis, adaptability, and reflection to determine the value, biases, and accuracy of generative AI content.

Outside the classroom, AI can help with organization. For example, a student balancing classes, sports, and a part-time job could use AI to create a weekly schedule or manage routine emails. This saves time and reduces stress, leaving energy for more complex projects or learning new skills. Adaptability in the future will come from knowing when to lean on AI and when to trust personal judgment.

Lifelong Learning: Staying Ahead in a Changing Job Market

Technology is changing jobs faster than ever. Skills that are useful today may need updating tomorrow. Lifelong learning helps workers stay prepared for new opportunities and be confident in a constantly evolving workplace. Here are some ways to keep learning.

- Develop soft skills: Communication, leadership, and teamwork are essential in almost every job and are hard for AI to replicate.
- Join community programs or clubs: Participating in debate, volunteering, or group projects build problem-solving and collaboration skills.
- Find a mentor or apprenticeship: Shadowing professionals and learning how they approach real-world challenges helps develop judgment and adaptability.
- Practice creativity and innovation: Activities like writing, public speaking, designing experiences, or creating original content strengthen skills that AI cannot fully imitate.
- Stay aware of industry trends: Following an insider's social media, reading articles, and attending workshops help people spot emerging opportunities and adapt before changes arrive.

Developing Hybrid Skills

The skills that will matter most in the future are hybrid skills—a mix of technical know-how and people-focused abilities. Hard skills are things people can measure and practice, like coding or analyzing data. Soft skills involve empathy, communication, and making thoughtful decisions. Teens who develop both types gain a set of abilities that AI cannot replace. For example, a student who listens well and studies health care technology could prepare for roles in patient counseling. Another student who enjoys art and learns psychology research methods could design apps and products that are both visually appealing and easy for people to use. A student who sharpens debate skills while learning AI tools for legal research could be ready for the evolving world of law.

"Highly specific, advanced technical skills are obviously important, but fundamental skills are actually really important too, if not more important."[27]

—Letian Zhang, associate professor of management and organizations at Northwestern University

"Highly specific, advanced technical skills are obviously important, but fundamental skills are actually really important too, if not more important,"[27] says Letian Zhang, associate professor of management and organizations at Northwestern University's Kellogg School of Management. His point highlights that mastering only technical abilities is not enough. Teens who blend hard and soft skills will be the ones shaping how AI fits into society.

Rethinking the Career Ladder

For much of the twentieth century, a typical career path was straightforward: finish college, get a job at one company, and stay there until retirement. That model began disappearing with the erosion of many manufacturing industries and the corporate restructuring practices in the 1980s. Workers had to adapt to layoffs, meaning they might change jobs several times to chase better financial prospects. New technologies, like AI and automation, are changing the nature of work even more rapidly; some careers that people train for today may no longer exist in just a few years. Even jobs that once seemed secure and exciting can shift or vanish almost overnight. In addition, new jobs generated by the AI boom may require workers to retrain to stay employable, and people might have to continually acquire new skills as jobs evolve in the face of the new technology.

When the internet first became popular, careers like web development and digital marketing were in high demand—modern, creative, and full of opportunity. Today, AI is beginning to handle some of the work in these fields, showing that even the newest, most sought-after jobs can be disrupted by innovation. Other examples from history include travel agents, telephone operators, and video store clerks—roles that were once stable but now mostly exist only in memory.

The idea of a single, linear career ladder no longer fits the modern workforce. Instead of moving steadily upward within one company, many people now navigate a series of lateral moves, freelance projects, and entirely new industries over the course of their careers. Some may go back to school, switch to a new field, or start their own business more than once. Success today is measured less by how long individuals stay at one job and more by how well they adapt and find opportunities in changing situations.

Even industries themselves are being redefined. Entire sectors, from transportation to media to retail, are evolving under the influence of AI, automation, and digital innovation. Careers that exist today may merge with others, split into new specializations, or disappear entirely. The "ladder" of work is becoming more like a network or web in which sideways moves and skill shifts are as important as upward promotions. One practical approach is for workers to stay curious, observe trends in the industries, and be willing to explore new paths, even if it means stepping sideways before moving forward.

The Rise of Continuous Learning

As technology changes the job market, education is no longer confined to the years spent preparing for an initial career. Completing a college degree is only the beginning, and even the focus of the higher education experience is changing. At the 2025 Engineering the Future with Artificial Intelligence event, Northeastern University President Joseph E. Aoun explained, "Every university should ask itself, 'Why do students come to us? Is it to get knowledge?' I can get knowledge anytime I want now—from AI chatbots, from many things. Students come for a different purpose—to integrate knowledge and to gain the experiential component."[28] His words show that learning today is not just about memorizing facts. It's about applying knowledge in real-life situations and developing skills that last. But his comment also demonstrates that learning is available outside of traditional classrooms and that graduates will likely use digital resources to learn new skills as career paths change in the face of automation.

Already, jobs are changing fast as the impacts of AI are felt. A software developer might need to learn about AI ethics, a designer could move into AI-enhanced virtual reality, and nurses or doctors may adapt to using AI tools to help diagnose patients. Lifelong learning lets people keep their skills in demand. However,

New jobs generated by the AI boom may require workers to retrain to stay employable, and people might have to continually acquire new skills as jobs evolve in the face of the new technology.

core skills that can be used in many areas—like problem-solving, creativity, and critical thinking—remain valuable because AI cannot replace them.

Teens interested in preparing for the modern work world can also take online classes, attend workshops, or join professional or hobby groups. Mentors and advisors can guide them and show how skills are used in future careers. Following industry news, watching webinars, and joining online discussions can help young people spot new technologies and opportunities. Personal projects—like creating an app, designing a website, or experimenting with electronics—also build practical skills and confidence.

The key takeaway is that learning never stops. By staying curious, trying new things, and adapting to change, students can turn challenges into opportunities. In a world where technology moves faster than ever, being able to learn, think critically, and use knowledge creatively will be among the most important skills for future careers.

High-Demand Fields to Watch

Some industries are growing faster than others. *The Future of Jobs Report 2025* indicates that fields like AI and big data, cybersecurity, and digital skills are especially fast growing. Cybersecurity specialists work to protect organizations from online threats, while data analysts use mathematical and computational tools to make sense of large sets of information. Students who build expertise in these subject areas are likely to find strong opportunities in the years ahead.

Health care is also being transformed by technology. New roles are emerging for professionals who can combine medical knowledge with AI, such as creating diagnostic tools or apps that help patients track their health.

Other fast-growing fields include renewable energy, robotics, and digital design. Students interested in engineering may pursue robotics, while those focused on environmental concerns may

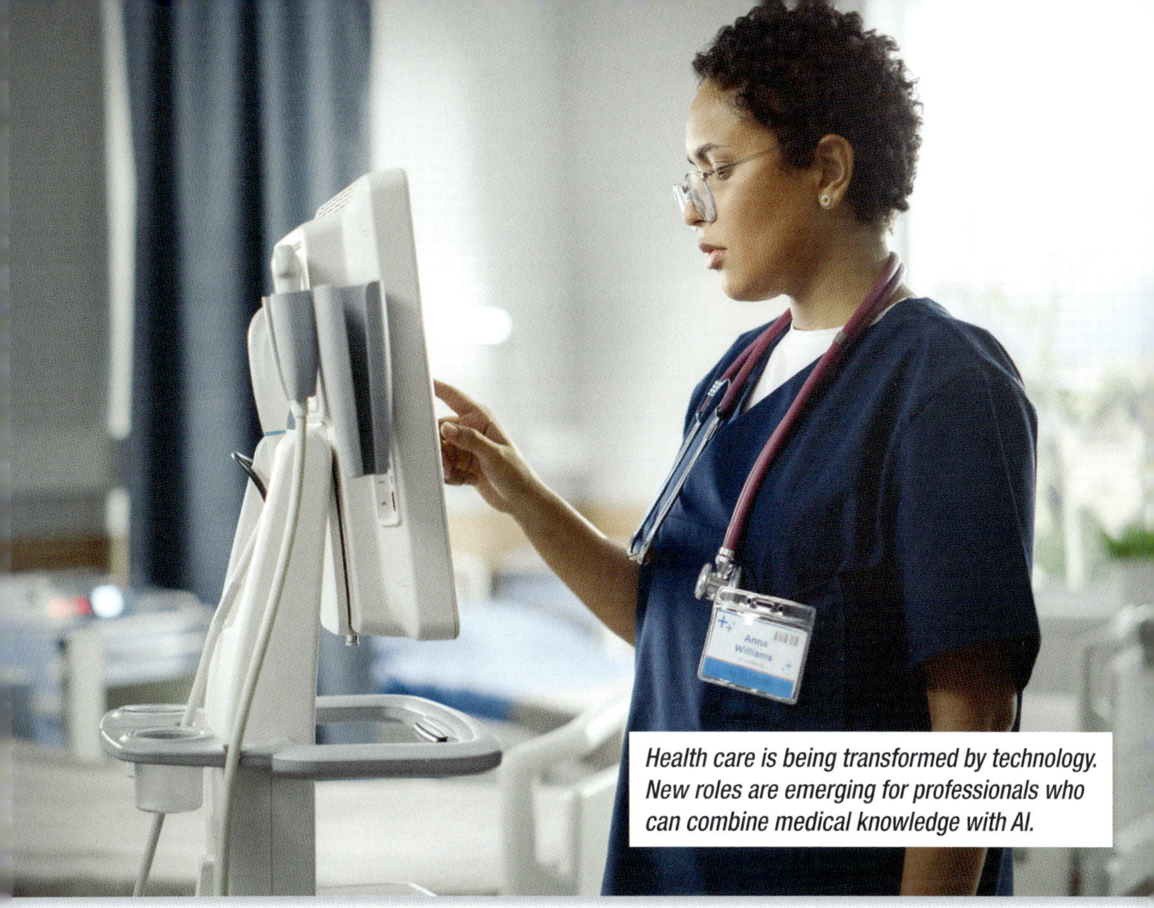

Health care is being transformed by technology. New roles are emerging for professionals who can combine medical knowledge with AI.

look toward sustainable energy systems. Even creative fields are evolving—virtual reality, game design, and interactive media are opening new career paths.

It is important for job seekers to notice where industries are expanding and think about how personal strengths can be combined with new technology. Those who do will be ready for careers that do not even exist yet.

Thinking About Entrepreneurship in an AI-Driven World

In a world where technology and AI are changing jobs, starting a business can be a smart move for young people. Entrepreneurship lets individuals create their own opportunities instead of waiting for traditional jobs to appear—or disappear. It also builds adaptability, problem-solving, and creativity, skills that are essential in an AI-powered economy.

Entrepreneurship has a big advantage because it lets people incorporate their own skills with the power and efficiency of AI tools. For example, a person could use AI to come up with new product ideas and test them quickly to see what customers like. A small business owner could use AI to track inventory or check sales, giving more time for planning, marketing, or building relationships with customers. In both cases, AI helps the work instead of replacing the human ideas that make a business special.

Starting a business can involve a wide range of skills—not just tech. Young people could sell handmade jewelry, start a tutoring service, design clothes or digital art, run a neighborhood delivery service, or even create social media content for small businesses. The key is to start small, test ideas, and learn from the experience. Online tools, social media, and apps make it easier than ever to research markets, advertise products, and manage tasks—even with limited resources.

History shows the power of starting early. When personal computers first became common, young entrepreneurs like Steve Jobs and Steve Wozniak of Apple began experimenting in garages, building and selling computers to hobbyists. Their early efforts helped create entirely new markets and eventually transformed

Hot Tech Careers Teens Can Explore

According to *The Future of Jobs Report 2025*, many fast-growing tech careers combine AI tools with strong human thinking skills. One major area is AI and big data. While AI can handle some coding or number-crunching, humans are needed to design systems, interpret results, and make decisions. Demand is growing for roles such as AI project managers, AI ethics coordinators, and data analysts.

Cybersecurity is another promising field. Hackers keep evolving, so humans are essential to protect digital systems. Careers like cybersecurity analyst, network security specialist, and security trainer are expected to grow steadily. Jobs in this field require spotting patterns, analyzing threats, and solving complex problems.

Fields that rely on digital skills, including design, content creation, and online marketing also continue to expand. AI can assist in these roles, but true creativity, strategy, and understanding audiences remain human strengths. Young people can explore user experience design, social media management, and digital marketing strategy.

the tech industry. In the AI-driven world today, starting a business gives young people the same chance to test ideas, learn from mistakes, and discover what people really need.

Entrepreneurship also teaches resilience. Running a business means handling uncertainty, making quick decisions, and adjusting plans when things change—skills that are useful whether the business succeeds or not. Even side projects provide experience, confidence, and practical knowledge that help in any career.

For teens entering the workforce in an AI-driven world, thinking like an entrepreneur—spotting opportunities, trying new ideas, and combining technology with human creativity—can give a major advantage. It is a way for individuals to take control of their career and shape a future that values both innovation and human talents.

SOURCE NOTES

Introduction: Unlike Anything Humanity Has Seen

1. Quoted in Hannah Mayer et al., "Superagency in the Workplace: Empowering People to Unlock AI's Full Potential," McKinsey & Company, January 28, 2025. www.mckinsey.com.
2. Quoted in Brent D. Griffiths, "Sam Altman Says We're Worried About the Wrong Part of the Workforce When It Comes to AI," Business Insider, August 12, 2025. www.businessinsider.com.

Chapter One: How AI Is Changing the Nature of Work

3. Monte Watkins, personal interview with the author.
4. Cody Pedersen, personal interview with the author.
5. Pedersen, interview.
6. Quoted in Iqbal Pittalwala, "How Is AI Influencing the Field of Medicine?," UC Riverside News, February 4, 2025. https://news.ucr.edu.
7. Quoted in Jeff John Roberts, "Will AI Hold Up in Court? Attorneys Say It's Already Changing the Practice of law," *Fortune*, June 26, 2025. https://fortune.com.
8. Quoted in Roger Dunaway, "New Tulane Study Finds Generative AI Can Boost Employee Creativity—but Only for Strategic Thinkers," Tulane University, June 6, 2025. https://news.tulane.edu.
9. Quoted in Eric Zhou, "Generative Artificial Intelligence, Human Creativity, and Art," *PNAS Nexus*, March 5, 2024. https://pmc.ncbi.nlm.nih.gov/articles/PMC10914360.
10. Pedersen, interview.
11. Mary Meeker et al., *Trends—Artificial Intelligence.* Bond, 2025. www.bondcap.com.

Chapter Two: Which Jobs Are Most at Risk and Why?

12. Quoted in Victor Tangermann, "Microsoft Releases List of Jobs Most and Least Likely to Be Replaced by AI," Futurism, July 29, 2025. https://futurism.com.

13. Quoted in George Jones and Rob Andrews, "Supermarket Cashiers 'Most at Risk of Being Replaced by AI,'" Yahoo! News, May 23, 2025. https://uk.news.yahoo.com.
14. Quoted in Rachel Curry, "Less Burnout for Doctors, Better Clinical Trials, Among the Benefits of AI in Health Care," CNBC, April 23, 2024. www.cnbc.com.
15. Quoted in Siddhant Adlakha, "The AI-Generated Movie *What's Next* Opens a Fresh Debate over AI Filmmaking," Polygon, April 24, 2025. www.polygon.com.
16. Quoted in Hannah Murphy, "Retraining Workers for the AI World," *Financial Times* (London, UK), June 3, 2024. www.ft.com.

Chapter Three: Which Jobs Are Least at Risk and Why?

17. Quoted in Zara Abrams, "Classrooms Are Adapting to the Use of Artificial Intelligence," *Monitor on Psychology*, January 1, 2025. www.apa.org.
18. Quoted in Deon J. Hampton, "Blue-Collar Jobs Are Gaining Popularity as AI Threatens Office Work," NBC News, August 16, 2025. www.nbcnews.com.
19. Quoted in Kit Eaton, "A 'Godfather' of the Internet Says You Should Become a Plumber." *Inc.*, June 17, 2025. www.inc.com.
20. Quoted in Richard Draycott, "Can AI Creative Ever Inspire Us like Human-Based Creativity?," The Drum, February 3, 2025. www.thedrum.com.
21. Quoted in CFA Institute, "In the Age of AI, It's Human Skills That Employers Want," April 15, 2025. www.cfainstitute.org.
22. Quoted in Michael Blanding, "To Lead Is Human: What Does Responsible Leadership Mean in the Age of AI?," *Darden Report*, June 27, 2024. https://news.darden.virginia.edu.
23. Quoted in Ellen Glover, "What Is the Eliza Effect?," Built In, July 14, 2023. https://builtin.com.
24. Quoted in Megan Cerullo, "New Study Sheds Light on What Kinds of Workers Are Losing Jobs to AI," CBS News, August 28, 2025. www.cbsnews.com.

Chapter Four: How AI Is Changing the Job Search Process

25. Quoted in Tor Constantino, "Why AI Is a Double-Edged Sword for 2025 Job Seekers—New Research," *Forbes*, March 11, 2025. www.forbes.com.

Chapter Five: How to Prepare: Skills for the AI-Powered Workplace

26. Quoted in *Virginia Tech Engineer*, "AI—the Good, the Bad, and the Scary," Fall 2023. https://eng.vt.edu.
27. Quoted in Jay Fitzgerald, "Why Soft Skills Still Matter in the Age of AI," Harvard Business School, June 24, 2025. www.library.hbs.edu.
28. Quoted in Cyrus Moulton, "AI in Higher Education Is Driving a Shift Toward Lifelong Learning, Northeastern President Says," Northeastern Global News, June 23, 2025. https://news.northeastern.edu.

FOR FURTHER RESEARCH

Books

John Allen, *Exploring Careers in AI*. ReferencePoint, 2025.

Ryan Harper, *AI-Proof Your Career: The Essential Survival Guide to Thriving in the Artificial Intelligence Revolution*. Rivanna Heights Media, 2024.

Stuart A. Kallen, *High-Tech Jobs in Robotics*. ReferencePoint, 2024.

Stephanie Sammartino McPherson, *Future Forward: Harnessing Artificial Intelligence*. Lerner, 2026.

Internet Sources

Suzanne Blake, "Most Workers Say AI Managers Would Be Better in Key Ways: Survey," *Newsweek*, September 4, 2024. www.newsweek.com.

Nia Bowers, "AI May Diagnose an Illness—but Only Trust Can Heal Healthcare," *USA Today*, September 11, 2025. www.usatoday.com.

Derek Gatopoulos, "AI Scientist Says 'Learning How to Learn' Will Be Next Generation's Most Needed Skill," ABC News, September 12, 2025. https://abcnews.go.com.

Alice Gibbs, "Top 40 Jobs Most Likely to Be Impacted by AI," *Newsweek*, July 31, 2025. www.newsweek.com.

Adam Mills, "AI Goes Mainstream as Nearly Half of Retail Brands Now Use It Weekly," *Newsweek*, September 11, 2025. www.newsweek.com.

PwC, "The Fearless Future: 2025 Global AI Jobs Barometer," PwC, June 3, 2025. www.pwc.com.

Thomas Westerholm, "Is Artificial Intelligence Dumbing Down Cancer Doctors?," *Newsweek*, August 15, 2025. www.newsweek.com.

Websites

Brookings Institution
www.brookings.edu
The Brookings Institution is a nonprofit organization devoted to in-depth research to improve policy and governance at local, national,

and global levels. Issues about AI make up an important part of its website content.

Center for AI Safety (CAIS)
https://safe.ai
The CAIS seeks to reduce AI risks through research, funding, and advocacy. The nonprofit organization aims to identify and address AI safety issues before they become significant concerns. Its website features information about AI risks, research projects, and more.

Hoover Institution
www.hoover.org
The Hoover Institution is an American public policy think tank that promotes economic liberty and prosperity, free enterprise, and limited government. Its website includes several articles that look at AI's rapid rise and life-changing possibilities, as well as its possible drawbacks.

Machine Intelligence Research Institute (MIRI)
https://intelligence.org
The MIRI seeks to align advanced AI with human interests. The institute works to ensure that the creation of smarter-than-human intelligence has a positive impact in the real world.

OpenAI
https://openai.com
OpenAI is an AI research and deployment company that aims to ensure that artificial intelligence benefits all of humanity. It is the developer of ChatGPT, a generative AI technology. Its website has information about the company and its research. Users can test ChatGPT on the website.

Partnership on AI
https://partnershiponai.org
The Partnership on AI is a nonprofit organization that promotes the responsible advancement and use of AI technology. Its website features articles, a blog, and other information about AI and its use.

INDEX

PICTURE CREDITS

Cover: WOSUNAN/Shutterstock

6: FatCamera/iStock
10: SDI Productions/iStock
14: New Africa/Shutterstock
18: Schimbator Studio/Shutterstock
23: Creativa Images/Shutterstock
27: Maury Aaseng
29: Mateg Kastlic/Shutterstock
31: PeopleImages/Shutterstock
35: gowithstock/Shutterstock
39: Demkat/Shutterstock
43: Maury Aaseng
45: Akarawut/Shutterstock
47: PonyWang/iStock
50: Prostock-studio/Shutterstock
51: tumka vodka/Shutterstock
54: Pixel-Shot/Shutterstock

ABOUT THE AUTHOR

Traci Pedersen has been writing for more than two decades, with thousands of published articles and a collection of science books for children. She lives in the Tampa Bay area of Florida and is the proud parent of three adult children.